D1538038

Have Heart

By David Eckstein

with Greg Brown

Published by Builder's Stone Publishing, LLC

7025 CR 46-A

Suite 1071 PMB 328

Lake Mary, Florida 32746-4753   (407) 549-5066

www.DavidEckstein.com

Printed in the United States of America.

Meet David Eckstein
Organ Donations Saved His Family

A Donate Life Organization

**Visit KidZone on our web site
at www.mts-stl.org to learn
how donation works, or go to
www.donatelife.net to see how to
enroll in your state donor registry.**

Dear Reader,

Like many families, David Eckstein's family has been touched by serious illness. They survive today because they were able to receive lifesaving organ transplants. Such transplants are only made possible when everyday people decide to be organ and tissue donors.

Please talk about organ and tissue donation with your family. Let them know how you feel. And if you would like to be a donor and help others in need, then please register wherever you live.

Just as David says, "ordinary people who have heart do amazing things".

We thank David Eckstein for the inspiring story of his life.

Mid-America Transplant Services

MID-AMERICA TRANSPLANT SERVICES

1139 Olivette Executive Pkwy.
St. Louis, MO 63132-3205
(314) 991-1661 • 1-888-376-4854

www.mts-stl.org

My name is David Eckstein, and you could call me a short shortstop. Ever since I picked up a bat, I've been the shortest player on the field. I stand just 5 feet, 7 inches (5'7"). Some Little Leaguers are taller than me.

Some baseball people said I'd never play in the Major Leagues. Some even said it to my face. Some said that I didn't have all five tools that scouts seek — hitting for average, hitting with power, speed, fielding, and arm strength.

It's true that I don't hit many home runs. I'm not the fastest on the field, and my arm is just strong enough. However, I always had the desire to be the best baseball player I could be since I was old enough to hold a bat. I never gave up, and I never lost heart. I knew I had to be my best at every level. This meant that I had to set goals for myself and continually work to improve my skills. As a result, I did become a Major League baseball player and I continued to set new goals and work hard. I was honored to play in two National League All-Star Games, play on the 2002 Anaheim Angels World Series championship team, and most recently, play on the 2006 St. Louis Cardinals World Series championship team where I was voted the Most Valuable Player.

Sometimes people tell me that I'm like the children's story *The Little Engine that Could*. I just keep trying and believing I can — having heart.

Someone's heart cannot be measured in inches, statistics, or seconds. Every day people who have heart do amazing things and beat the odds. To understand what I mean by having heart, you must first understand my family and how I grew up.

3

My parents, Whitey and Pat Eckstein, were born in Newark, New Jersey, in the same hospital, and baptized in the same church. Yet, their families did not know each other. Remarkably, both of my parents' families moved to the same street in DeBary, Florida, where they became friends.

They both graduated from the University of Florida and married on June 8, 1968. Both became school teachers — my father teaching high school history and my mother teaching elementary school. My parents settled in Sanford, where I was born on January 20, 1975.

My father wanted a large family because he grew up as an only child and always wished for brothers and sisters. So, a large family is what my parents had. My mother gave birth to five children — three boys (Ken, Rick, and me) and two girls (Christine and Susan) - all within 5½ years.

I was the youngest of the five, the baby of the family. Soon after my birth Mom could tell something was different about the son she still calls "D." Mom always had short, fat babies. I was short and thin. Also, instead of gaining weight like babies are supposed to do after they are born, I lost weight.

Sanford

Orlando

Miami

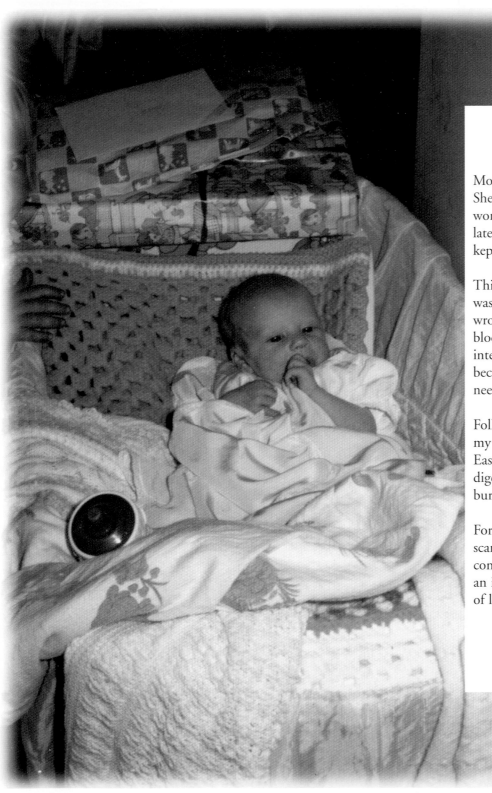

Mom knew in her heart something was wrong. She took me to a pediatrician, who told her she worried too much and sent us home. A few days later we went to the emergency room because I kept throwing up.

This time a different doctor told Mom that she was right. Something was wrong—terribly wrong. I had a blockage in my stomach. The blockage prevented food from entering my intestines to be digested. I was throwing up because the food had no other place to go. So, I needed emergency surgery to save my life.

Following the surgery by Dr. Charles Park, Jr., my mom prayed at my crib for a week. Then, on Easter Sunday, Mom got a sign that told her my digestive system started working. I passed gas, burped, and screamed for food.

For the first time in my life, I felt hunger! My scar from the surgery is only a few inches now, as compared to the width of my body when I was an infant. It is a constant reminder of the miracle of life and how blessed I am to be alive.

My parents will tell you I was born loving baseball. As a 2-year-old, I'd sit and watch a whole game on television, barely moving a muscle. By age 3, I knew the names of players. At age 4, I could remember entire team rosters. My dad loved watching the Atlanta Braves games on TV, and so did I.

My favorite player was Dale Murphy, who to this day I consider to be a great baseball player as well as a great person. In 1977, we went to Atlanta to see the Braves play. This was my first family vacation.

We did not go on many family vacations because we did not have much extra money. However, if we did go on vacation, we all went together as a family. My parents always said if one member of our family couldn't go on vacation, nobody would.

Another memorable family trip for me was when we traveled north to Cooperstown, New York, to see the Baseball Hall of Fame. I was 5 years old. I still remember having my picture taken in front of Mickey Mantle's display and hitting in the batting cages. I was in awe with the whole experience, so you can imagine how honored and thrilled I was when the Baseball Hall of Fame asked for the cleats I wore during the 2002 World Series and my game hat as the MVP of the 2006 World Series. It is a tradition for the Hall of Fame to ask for the MVP's hat.

From Cooperstown, my family traveled to New York City and watched a game in Yankee Stadium. We were in the upper deck near the left-field line. What I remember most about the game was seeing Yankee catcher Rick Cerone hit a home run and watching Yankee Manager Billy Martin come out of the dugout and argue a call. Because of this trip, I knew that baseball was what I wanted to do more than anything else in the world.

My family lived in a modest 4-bedroom house in Sanford, which is about 35 miles from Walt Disney World. It was always a special day to go to Disney World, but it was, at most, only a once-a-year treat. Instead, my backyard was my amusement park.

I first started playing baseball in our backyard with my brother, Rick. We would make up games to try to improve our skills. To improve our hitting, Rick and I played "challenge rounds" with either tennis balls or racquetballs. We would stand approximately 20 feet from each other and the pitcher would throw the ball as hard as possible challenging the hitter to make contact.

Rick and I show off our catch during my first fishing trip.

To enhance our fielding, we hit hard sharp grounders to each other from the same 20-foot distance. Once done with our practice, we would play games.

As we grew older, Rick and I played baseball with friends in the neighborhood. Although the guys were at least two years older than me, I would still tag along and play with the older kids. I pushed myself to keep up with the older guys. So right from the start, I was the little guy trying to prove himself.

I have a soft heart for animals, especially dogs. I've always enjoyed being around animals and having pets.

The backyard at my parents' house is a pet cemetery. We didn't put gravestone markers in the dirt, but buried there are five family dogs—Lady, Ruby, Rusty, Pete, and Queenie—13 puppies, which didn't survive birth, a guinea pig (Coffee), three cockatiels, (Baby, Katie, and Hansie) and a cat named Francis.

We always had pets around our house. We gave our pets love and respect. They were part of our family. Rusty, an English Springer, grew up with me and died of old age in 1996. A piece of my childhood died with him.

Queenie, a black mixed lab with a white chest, was a runaway. She was skinny and neglected. I told Mom about this poor dog and how it needed a home. I begged Mom to let us keep her. When she said yes, she thought I had the dog with me. But I didn't. I had to go run the neighborhood to find her.

Ruby gave us a scare during the only hurricane that damaged our house. Hurricane "David" hit Florida in 1980. It knocked down our fence and Ruby ran away. Within a few days, she came home and weeks later gave birth to 15 puppies. Only two survived: Tippy and Duke.

The summer before first grade I got my chance to play tee-ball. When the coaches handed out our mustard-yellow uniforms, I rushed to a restroom to put it on. Mom says my face lit up with excitement. My pants were on backwards, my jersey was buttoned unevenly and hanging out, and my hat was on crooked. Mom wished she had taken a picture. I promptly ran through a puddle and splattered my uniform with mud, but I was ready to play my first "real" game!

The next season Mom did not want me to play tee-ball again because she felt I was too advanced for it. Rick's Pony Baseball coach, Coach Suggs, agreed and let me serve as the batboy for his Mustang team.

I took it seriously and hustled from the dugout to the plate to pick up the bats. I watched every play and soaked in all the details of the game. Best of all, I got to practice with the older team and my brother Rick.

My relationship with Rick and the rest of my family emphasizes the foremost rule in the Eckstein household: "family first."

My father would always say:
"Family is the most important thing."
"You can always depend on family."
"We do not do anything unless it is as a family."

This meant that I spent a lot of time playing together with my brothers and sisters, sharing a room with my brothers, and going everywhere as a family.

Eckstein's rules of the house

- Mind our parents.
- Family comes first.
- Everyone shares.
- Be respectful of all adults; address adults "Yes, Sir" or Yes, Ma'am."
- No talking back.
- Say your prayers every day and go to church on Sundays.
- Give 100 percent in whatever you do.
- No pouting or complaining.

My parents were always home with us when they were not at work. Many Friday nights, particularly during Lent, we had cheese pizza from our favorite pizza place and would watch TV as a family.

On Saturdays, we would go out for dinner. Afterwards, we would all go to the mall to play video games while Mom and Dad watched. I remember these times not because anything extraordinary happened, but because how happy I felt just doing ordinary things with the family. So, although I did not grow up rich in money, I grew up rich in values.

When it came to food we were never forced to eat something we didn't like. Mom often made three different meals as we had different favorites. A taste I hate to this day is ketchup. I eat hamburgers plain.

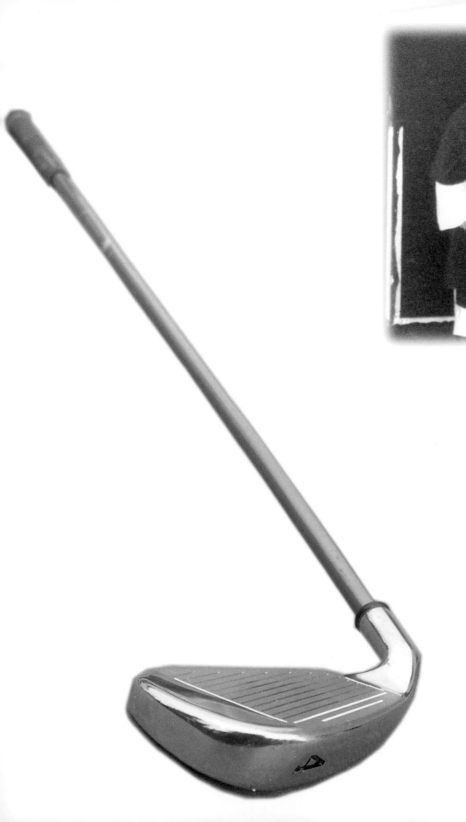

Our family played well together. We had a pool table. We put on family plays. We played "Let's Make a Deal," using pillows for curtains. In the summer we also played golf together often attending the summer golf clinics.

When I was 2 a golf club sent me back to the hospital. Rick was practicing his golf swing in our front yard. I walked into his swing and got clubbed in the head. I had a gash in my head, and my blond hair turned ketchup red. Mom rushed me to the emergency room. When she saw the doctor stitching my wound, she passed out. I came home giggling.

Ken and my sisters didn't play team sports. They took some gymnastics classes but never competed. Ken and Christine competed in public speaking contests and had top grades. My sister Susan excelled in the classroom as well. Rick and I followed in their footsteps and earned top grades.

Happy Acres Kindergarten and Child Care in Sanford, Florida. I was 4 years old. That's me in the first row, wearing the yellow shirt.

When it came to school, there was no arguing about the importance of education. With both of my parents being teachers, there were no excuses for poor study habits or bad grades. My parents usually knew my grades before I did. I knew that if there ever was a problem, my dad would march right into my classroom and discuss the problem in front of the entire class. Fortunately for me, I enjoyed going to school, did well, and that never happened.

My handwriting is what gave me a little trouble in school. Everyone in my family has perfect handwriting except me. Compared to them, mine is sloppy. Mom always called it chicken scratch. Whenever my family hears someone comment about how neat my autograph looks, we all look at each other and smile.

Being one of the shortest people in my class was not a problem. All of my older brothers and sisters were short so they experienced all the "short jokes" before me.

We all learned to laugh along rather than get upset. In fact, my brother Ken used his shortness to his advantage by being elected president of his 9th grade class with the slogan "4-foot-9 vote Eckstein."

I learned a person's size does not determine what they can accomplish. What counts is the size of a person's heart — the attitude on the inside to be their best — that is the true measure of a person.

Things I don't do well

- Handwriting
- Singing
- Anything mechanical

17

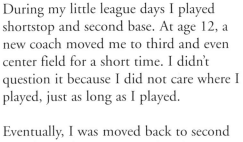

Can you find me in this picture? I'm in the front row, second from the right.

During my little league days I played shortstop and second base. At age 12, a new coach moved me to third and even center field for a short time. I didn't question it because I did not care where I played, just as long as I played.

Eventually, I was moved back to second and that is the position I played throughout high school and college.

The whole family got involved with the baseball games — except Dad. Mom helped keep score and Ken, Christine, and Susan cheered from the stands. But Dad stayed home. Why? Because he wanted Little League baseball to be fun for me and Rick. Believe me, not one thing that happens in Little League baseball will determine if someone makes it to the Major Leagues. Dad knew this and didn't want to rob us of our joy by taking Little League too seriously. However, Dad was very interested. After every game, Rick and I would give him a full, pitch-by-pitch game report.

Courtesy of Tommy Vincent/Seminole Herald

Courtesy of Tommy Vincent/Seminole Herald

I experienced my first "World Series" when I was in high school. Our Seminole Pony Baseball team made it to the Colt World Series for 15 and 16 year olds in Lafayette, Indiana. We were knocked out in the first round. I remember teammates crying when we lost our final game. I didn't cry. To me, winning is doing your best regardless of the outcome. Sometimes you win the game and sometimes you lose. It's part of the process of baseball and of life — learning from your experiences and moving on. However, when you give 100 percent, you can move on knowing you had played your best.

When I did cry, I cried over something completely different. I was in the 7th grade when life changed dramatically. My sister, Susan, who was 16 at the time, looked run down. She just wasn't acting like herself. Mom felt in her heart that something was wrong. Mom took Susan to the doctor for a checkup.

The doctor discovered that her kidneys had failed. Kidneys, located in the lower back, are needed to cleanse the blood in our bodies. She was rushed in an ambulance to Shands Hospital in Gainesville, Florida, about 100 miles away.

For 11 months, Susan fought for her life. She did dialysis to cleanse her blood. She needed a kidney transplant. Mom was a perfect match, so she gave Susan one of her kidneys on November 29, 1988.

On December 16th, Susan and Mom were finally released from the hospital. Everyone was thankful. The long ordeal seemed to be over. However, as Mom and Susan arrived home, the phone rang. It was Susan's doctor.

Mom asked, "What's wrong with Susan now?"

He replied, "It's not Susan - it's Christine."

The Ecksteins go to Washington: (from left) Mom, Rick, Dad, Ken, Me, Christine, and Susan.

Lab tests showed that Christine was in kidney failure, and she needed to start dialysis as soon as possible. The news seemed almost unbelievable.

Just when we thought we had gotten our life back, we were starting all over again. This was a time I remember crying.

Ten months later, my brother Ken began dialysis as well.

Despite our family misfortune, nobody blamed God or turned bitter or asked: "Why us?" Our faith taught us things happen for a reason. We might not know what that reason is, but our job is to move forward —taking it one day at a time and doing the best we can.

Ken, Christine, and Susan did dialysis four times a day, yet Ken needed more. He was hooked up to a machine for 10 hours a day. I can remember watching as they bravely went on with their lives never using their condition as an excuse. In fact, they all continued with their schooling. During his dialysis, Ken went to Washington, D.C., to serve as a Congressional intern.

Previously, as a high school junior, Ken served as a Congressional page. He was voted "Most Outstanding Page of the Year." We were all so proud of him. We took a family trip to Washington, D.C., to see him receive the award which, coincidentally, was given on his 16th birthday, June 13, 1986.

Christine was on dialysis for 31 months, and Ken was on dialysis for 17 months when, in July of 1991, both were called for kidney transplants. Incredibly, Ken and Christine were called only four days apart from each other. What a miracle of life it was, especially considering that some people die waiting to receive a transplant. Thankfully, both transplants were successful. Fortunately, neither Rick nor I have kidney problems.

Living through this difficult time solidified our family ties. It also made us stronger and more determined to live our lives to the fullest.

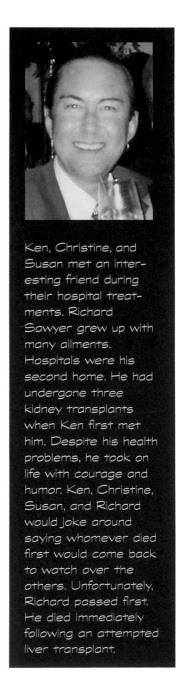

Ken, Christine, and Susan met an interesting friend during their hospital treatments. Richard Sawyer grew up with many ailments. Hospitals were his second home. He had undergone three kidney transplants when Ken first met him. Despite his health problems, he took on life with courage and humor. Ken, Christine, Susan, and Richard would joke around saying whomever died first would come back to watch over the others. Unfortunately, Richard passed first. He died immediately following an attempted liver transplant.

21

By the time I reached high school, things were almost normal in our house. School and baseball were my focus. I lived a pretty boring life. I didn't smoke or drink alcohol and didn't go to parties.

I had a circle of close friends and we did things together. My dad always said, "Show me a man's friends and I'll show you the man." One of my close friends then, and now, is Terry Tillis, a Captain in the U.S. Army. He fought in Iraq serving in the 4th Infantry out of Fort Hood, Texas.

He once gave me a birthday card that said, "Sorry I couldn't buy you anything because I am down to my last dollar." Inside the card was a dollar bill. The gesture exemplified Terry's giving spirit and his great sense of humor.

On my 16th birthday, Dad gave me a great gift — my most embarrassing moment in high school. He came into my Latin class and sang, "Happy Birthday." Then he sang "Sweet Sixteen and Has Never Been Kissed."

Despite my embarrassment at the time, I look back on this memory warmly, remembering how special my dad tried to make me feel. When I become a father, I might end up doing the same thing.

During high school, and even today, I try to make my parents proud of me.

If you are faced with a decision, and you don't know what's right or wrong, ask yourself this: "Will my choice make my parents proud of me?" If the answer is yes, that's almost always the right choice.

Eckstein's hustle helps Seminole to title

☐ The junior second baseman went 4-for-9 with an inside-the-park homer in the state tourney.

By Jill Cousins
OF THE SENTINEL STAFF

David Eckstein has a difficult time describing his love for baseball. But when he takes the field, his exuberance tells the story.

Eckstein, Seminole's junior second baseman, innings. He position. after the one-man ates with

talk to Da- the time," aid. "He gets me. He really when they're 't down many ves 100 percent

thin. He's that type

Photo by Mindy Schauer/Sentinel

If you are faced with a decision and you don't know what's right or wrong, ask yourself this: "Will my choice make my partents proud of me?"

22

The highlight of my high school baseball career came in my junior year when my high school baseball team won the state championship — the first in the school's history. This was an incredible accomplishment because the Fighting Seminoles had losing seasons the previous 10 years and we finished last in our league the year before. I felt like I was on top of the world. With this win, my focus turned to playing well my senior year and earning a college scholarship to a Division I school.

Things, however, did not turn out the way I had hoped my senior year. My high school team came within one out of going to the state championship tournament and no Division I school offered me a baseball scholarship. So I had to come up with a plan to play Division I ball.

My prom date, Heather Youmans, and I smile for the camera. I wore a crown because my class voted me Prom King.

Following in my family's footsteps and my childhood dream, I became a Gator. My challenge now was to try to make the team as a walk-on. So in August, before fall baseball tryouts, Christine went with me to meet the Florida baseball coaches. We asked about the tryout dates. I was pleased when the coaches offered to let me use the batting cages until the tryouts. Every day I worked out in the cages on my own. I wasn't allowed on the field, where returning team members were running and playing catch on their own. When the official practice started, a second baseman suddenly transferred to another school. The Gators needed a backup second baseman for scrimmages.

Because I was the only person who hit in the cages every day, the coaches invited me to scrimmage. They didn't give me a uniform, but I did get a hat. That was enough for me. I made the team as a walk-on.

I did not play much my freshman year. However, in my sophomore year, I earned the starting position at second base. I played well enough to earn scholarships for my junior and senior years.

Rick, who also played baseball, transferred to UF my junior year and made the team. At that time, all five of us were UF students. To make ends meet, we lived together to save money for my parents, who supported us all through school. True to our upbringing, all money was pooled together. We even shared a car and had to work out pick-up and drop-off schedules. Once again the family had to work together in order to move forward.

During my college baseball career, I set five school records and twice made the All-America Academic Team. My favorite memory was making it to the College World Series in Omaha, Nebraska, and playing in the semifinals with my brother Rick. Late in the game Rick was moved from left field to third base, and we turned a double-play together — a classic Eckstein-to-Eckstein moment — and one that I'll always cherish. The team finished third, which made us all very proud and thankful.

My Florida records include:

- Runs scored — 222
- Hits — 276
- Hit by pitch — 41
- Assists — 671
- Double plays — 142
- 23 career home runs

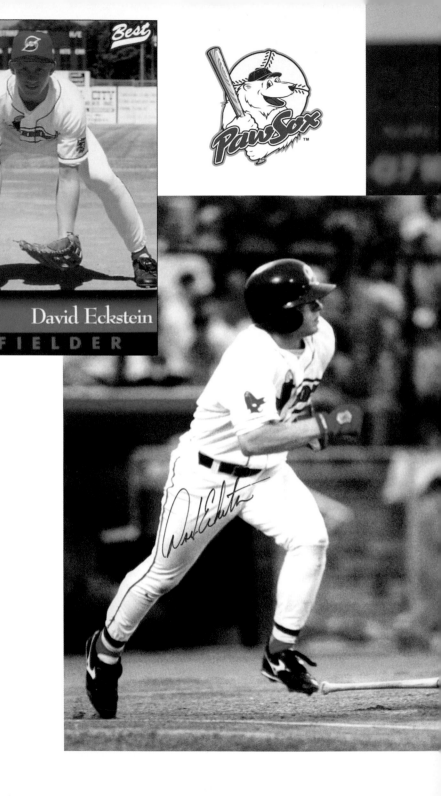

David Eckstein

INFIELDER

After my last game as a UF Gator, a few Major League teams called. Some promised to pick me in the baseball draft. Some thought I might be taken in the 10th through 15th rounds.

The Boston Red Sox picked me in the 19th round. About 500 players were picked ahead of me, but I was grateful that my name was called. I was excited to sign my first professional contract, which paid a $1,000 bonus. The scout who signed me said I would have to prove myself all over again (he told my dad I'd probably play a few years in the minors and make a good coach). But, I was used to proving myself.

My first day in the minor leagues, I was stopped at the gate. Shawn Smith, the Lowell Spinners' General Manager, said: "Excuse me, son, can I help you?"

"I'm a second baseman," I answered.

"Oh, I thought you were someone's little brother," he said.

People still say I look very young and that does not bother me at all. It is a reminder that looks can be deceiving – it's what's on the inside that decides who a person is and what a person can accomplish. Shawn and I still laugh about our first introduction and have remained friends.

For the first four games in Short Season A Ball, I sat the bench waiting for my chance to play. When I got that chance, I went after it 100 percent. As a result, I had a great season and the manager said I deserved the team's Most Valuable Player award.

Boston's upper management overruled and decided the award should go to their star draft pick. Following family rules, I did not pout. Although winning the MVP award would have been a great honor, it was not necessary for me to win in order to continue striving to do my best.

Following my first professional season, I moved through Boston's minor league system. I enjoyed the minor leagues, and I met some great friends along the way.

Although some aspects of being in the minor leagues were tough—like the 14-hour bus rides—it was nothing compared to what my brother and sisters had to deal with in coping with their kidney failure. They did it with a positive attitude. So I never complained.

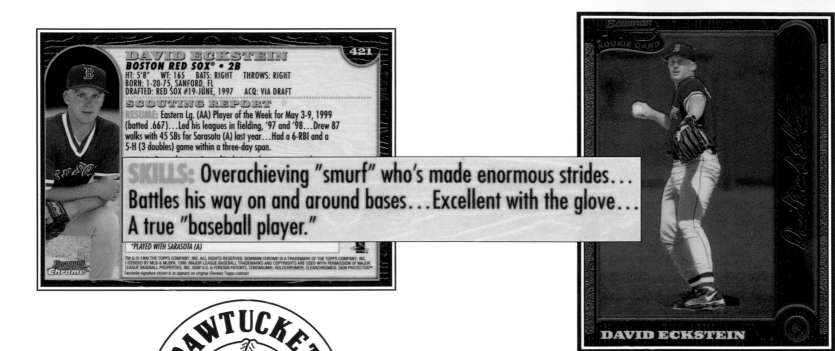

DAVID ECKSTEIN

My toughest experience in the minor leagues happened when I was on the AAA Red Sox team in Pawtucket, Rhode Island. The hitting instructors insisted I'd never play in the Big Leagues with my swing. So they changed it.

I tried hitting their way for 100 plate appearances —I really tried. But I had just nine hits in the 100 at-bats, and two were bunt hits. After every game I called home and talked about the game with my dad. I didn't tell my parents or family about the hitting change. I'm a pretty quiet guy and didn't want to complain.

But my career was in free-fall, and I did not know what to do. Finally, I told my family about what had happened. The next day my brother Rick flew to Columbus, Ohio, to have a heart-to-heart talk with me. Because of the hitting adjustments, I had forgotten my old swing. Rick knew my swing and helped me get back to my old self. After talking with Rick, I knew what I had to do.

I apologized to the Boston coaches and said, "I need to do what I need to do for myself. I need to get back to being me." So I went back to hitting my way, and I began hitting the ball! Unfortunately, it was too late. The Red Sox put me on waivers near the end of the season, and it appeared my baseball career was over.

I talked with everyone in my family over the phone and they all encouraged me not to give up. "You can't quit now," they all said. "Someone will give you another chance." Sure enough, that chance came thanks to the Anaheim Angels. The Angels picked me up and sent me to their AAA club in Edmonton for the final 15 games of the season. Having regained my old swing, I finished strong with a .346 batting average and three home runs. It earned me an invitation to Anaheim's 2001 Spring Training camp.

Coming into camp, I knew I had to prove myself and do everything possible to make the club. However, I needed an opportunity to do that. That opportunity came about when the starting second baseman, Adam Kennedy, broke his hand. As a result of this injury, Adam would miss the rest of spring training and the first week of the regular season leaving the second base position up for grabs. I was determined to make it mine until Adam returned for this was my opportunity to make the club.

As camp was winding down and things were going well, I heard the heartbreaking news that our family friend, Richard, died. I felt a heavy heart. Although Richard never played sports because of all of his medical problems, he would jokingly warn me, "You better play well, or I'll kick your butt." He always took an interest in my baseball career and would say, "I'll watch over you. Any coach I need to see? I'll get you a chance to play. The rest is up to you."

I would laugh at Richard when he said such things; however, I knew in spirit, he would always watch over me.

Just two days later, right before the first pitch of a spring training game, I was sitting on the bench with the team, and Manager Mike Scioscia leaned over and said softly: "I just wanted to let you know you made the team." My heart wanted to burst with excitement. However, I kept my emotions to myself. As soon as I got back to my hotel, I called my family with the great news: "I MADE THE TEAM!!!

Opening day 2001 in Arlington, Texas, is where my Major League dream came true. I was the starting second baseman batting ninth for the Anaheim Angels. During the game, I recorded my first Major League hit against Kenny Rogers. Things continued to go well for the next six days. Knowing Adam Kennedy was due to return, I was prepared to be sent down to AAA.

However the strangest thing happened. Alfredo Griffin, our infield coach convinced Manager Mike Scioscia to move me to shortstop. He believed I could learn the position while playing at the Major League level even though I had only played the position in 23 games during my minor league career. This rarely happens in the Major Leagues. Fortunately, during the offseason, I had practiced playing shortstop with my brother Rick, just in case something opened up. I knew this opportunity was a sign from Richard and my big chance to prove myself.

Donald Miralle/Getty Images

During my first year, I set a rookie record by being hit 21 times.

AP/Wide World Photos

30

Now I was in the Major Leagues, and I wanted to prove that I belonged. Dad always told us to walk into a room like you own the place. Not in an arrogant way, but with a quiet confidence. The difference between the two is the first you have to tell people how confident you are, and in the second, you show it by your actions.

Even though we finished 41 games out of first place in the American League West race in 2001, I felt we were on the doorstep of something great. We all knew we could improve if we kept a positive attitude. Having heart is easy when everything is going your way. The true test comes when things aren't.

We opened the 2002 season with a 6-14 start, which was not good, to say the least. One thing that helped early on was a meeting Mr. Scioscia called during our first series in Seattle. He told us he believed in us. He said we had the talent to be champions, and I knew he was right.

Soon after, we started turning our season around by winning 21 of 24 games. We started to believe we could come from behind in any game. For the season we had 43 comeback wins. I even hit three grand slams, two on back-to-back days. Those were surprises since I never had hit a grand slam before.

AP/Wide World Photos

AP/Wide World Photos

As August slipped away, the Oakland A's won a record 20 games in a row. We kept our focus on what we could do and stayed in the race. Finally, we needed just one win to clinch a wildcard playoff spot. But we lost four straight days, giving the Seattle Mariners a chance to catch us.

Reporters reminded us that in 1995, the Angels blew an 11-game lead over the Seattle Mariners in August and missed the playoffs. However, we were a different team, and what happened in the past was the past.

When we beat the Texas Rangers to reach the playoffs, Scott Spiezio celebrated by picking me up and tossing me into a tub of ice water.

Even though our team lacked playoff experience, we supported each other, and knew we could win. Losing the first game of every series in the playoffs didn't dampen our spirits.

New York, the team with the most World Series wins (26), was our first test. We passed the test. Next came the

Minnesota Twins, where a three-homerun performance by Adam Kennedy in Game 5 propelled us to the World Series.

Both series ended with me catching the final out. After the last game, I gave my dad both game-ending baseballs.

Mom, Christine, Susan, Rick, and my nephew Kenny came to California for Games 6 and 7 of the World Series. They all piled into my apartment, some sleeping on the floor in sleeping bags. This felt like home. Unfortunately, my dad, a Sanford City Commissioner, could not come because he said he had important meetings to attend. But we spoke every day and he was with me in my heart. Looking back, I now know that, although he had important meetings, Dad also didn't feel well because he was in the beginning stages of kidney failure. He did not tell me how he felt because he did not want me to worry or lose my focus.

The World Series played out in perfect drama. Every pitch seemed to mean everything. Barry Bonds put on a gigantic display of power with four home runs. The Angels' shining moment came in Game 6.

People always ask me now if I gave up when our team was down 5-0 in the seventh inning. No I didn't. I knew we needed to make a move soon. I kept thinking, "We have to find a way to get one run. The hardest thing is the first run."

Scott Spiezio's three-run homer gave us the lift we needed and a two-run double by Troy Glaus gave us the win.

I started off Game 7 with a rare base running mistake. I didn't get back to second base on a line-drive flyout. Despite my mistake, I knew that I had to put it behind me and stay focused on the moment. By remaining focused and not letting my mistake affect my thinking, I hit a leadoff single in the third inning that started a three-run rally, capped by Garret Anderson's bases-loaded double. Neither team scored the rest of the game. We won 4-1.

My most memorable moment about the post-game celebrations was having my family on the field with me after the game. We hugged with joyful sighs of relief while a wonderful sea of red fans waved and cheered with Halo Sticks. I'll always treasure that moment. During the on-field celebration, I called Dad with my cell phone to share the experience with him. I also called my high school coach, Mike Powers, and thanked him for all he had done for me. Later, I gave Dad my World Series ring.

The offseason held a few surprises. I was invited to play on a Major League Baseball All-Star team that toured Japan. The team needed a bullpen catcher so I told them my brother, Rick, could do the job. They gave him a chance, and he joined us. Together, Rick and I had an amazing trip, and we both felt incredibly privileged to be among some of the best players in baseball.

After returning home from Japan, I received an invitation from George Will to have dinner with President George W. Bush and other baseball people at the White House. I was able to bring one guest, so I brought my Mom. She was thrilled. Not only did we have dinner with the President, we also had a tour of the White House by President Bush himself! It was an awesome experience and one we will never forget.

After enjoying these special moments, I had to get back to the business of preparing physically and mentally for the next season. During the offseason, I run, lift weights, practice fielding and hitting. I do all of this as part of a daily routine with my brother Rick. Rick and I have a special bond. He shares my passion for baseball and understands that playing good baseball requires practice and discipline. Rick has always been there for me from playing in our backyard to today. As a player, no one knows me better than Rick.

For me to be successful, it starts with being prepared physically and mentally. I run, lift weights, practice fielding and hitting during the winter. Also, I get my mind focused on the game and thinking positively on the challenges that I must meet in the upcoming season.

37

The 2003 season was a rough year for me. I got sick in preseason with food poisoning. The day I came back, I strained my back. I constantly fought injuries the whole season. Our team had its share of injuries, too, and we didn't even make it to the playoffs that year. We were all disappointed, including the players, the coaches, the organization and the fans.

It was also a difficult year for my family. In March 2003, Dad was told that his kidney function was below 10 percent and that he had to go on dialysis. On April 29, 2003, Dad began his 28-month dialysis ordeal. Dad needed a kidney transplant, and did all the tests necessary to be placed on the cadaveric kidney waiting list.

Rick and I offered one of our kidneys, but Dad would not accept either. He said we had to save our kidneys for our future children, including nieces and nephews. We now know that two of Christine's children, David and Kenny, have been diagnosed with renal disease. They are currently on medication to slow the progression of this disease.

When the community learned that Dad needed a kidney, ten family friends stepped forward to offer one of theirs. The whole family was moved by the incredible generosity of these people. Unfortunately, none were determined to be a viable candidate. This worried us because we were not sure how long Dad would survive on dialysis. Dialysis was taking its toll on Dad's body. He was retaining large amounts of fluid that caused him to go into congestive heart failure on three occasions. So, his wait continued on the cadaveric kidney donor list.

Something wonderful did happen in September of 2003. I met my future wife, Ashley Drane. Ashley is an actress known for her TV roles on *Blue Collar TV* and *That's So Raven*. Coincidentally, she grew up in Orlando, Florida, not far from my home in Sanford. In pursuit of her acting career, Ashley moved to Los Angeles. For two years, Ashley's friends encouraged her to meet me because they thought we would make a good match. Ashley finally decided to ask me to accompany her to a red carpet event. Ashley's publicist contacted the Angels, and word got to me that an "angelic" young woman wanted to meet me. With such a recommendation, I decided to meet Ashley. I am so glad I did because we have been together ever since.

During the 2003 offseason, I went through what is called salary arbitration. When a team and player can't agree on the player's salary, an arbitration panel is brought in to decide on a fair salary. Each side presents their case to the arbitration panel. Although this process can be confrontational, it is part of the business of baseball and cannot be taken personally. My agents Ryan Gleichowski and Marc Pollack of Sports One Athlete Management, Inc. made an excellent presentation to the arbitration panel that included their statistical research of how I compared with other shortstops in Major League Baseball. The arbitrators agreed that the money I was asking for was fair and that I had earned it.

The 2004 season was a good one for me. I was healthy and led all Major League shortstops with my fielding percentage of .988 with only 6 errors. I was very happy because my father considers fielding percentage as the most important statistic. The excitement of the year culminated with the Angels winning the American League Western Division and making the playoffs.

Unfortunately, the Red Sox swept us. They then went on to break their 86-year-old "Curse of the Bambino" by overcoming history and the St. Louis Cardinals to win their first World Series since 1918.

AP/Wide World Photos

As it turned out, 2004 became the last year I would play in Anaheim. In December, I was not tendered a contract by the Angels. I was now a free agent. While I was disappointed that I would not be playing with the Angels anymore, I realized that, once again, this was part of the business of baseball. I was thankful to the Angels organization for giving me the opportunity to be a Major League player. Also, I was appreciative, and always will be appreciative, to the fans who supported me.

Almost immediately, my agent Ryan began receiving e-mails from other teams expressing their interest in me. In particular, the St. Louis Cardinals made it known that they wanted me and the player that I am. I was ecstatic for I felt the Cardinals would be a perfect fit. Within a couple of days I had agreed to terms to become a St. Louis Cardinal.

My first appearance in St. Louis was for Winter Warm-Up, a charity signing event to raise money for the St. Louis Cardinals' Foundation, Cardinal Care. When I walked on stage, the fans gave me a standing ovation. Considering the rich tradition of shortstops in Cardinals' history, I was overwhelmed and grateful by such a response. This extraordinary welcome by the fans confirmed that I had made the right choice by signing with the Cardinals.

AP Photo/Tom Gannam

I returned home to Sanford to prepare for my first spring training as a Cardinal, but before I did that I had to prepare myself for one more thing, engagement. I proposed to my girlfriend Ashley on February 4th, 2005, at Walt Disney World. She said, "Yes!" The wedding was set for the following November.

During my first season with the Cardinals, I had the honor of being voted onto the 2005 National League All-Star Team. It was the second surprise I received that summer. The first surprise was that a kidney donor for Dad had been found.

In January 2005, Lori Vaughan, my brother Ken's best friend, told Ken she wanted to be tested to donate a kidney to my dad. She and Ken decided to keep most of the testing a secret so as to surprise Dad if she was a suitable candidate and not disappoint him if it didn't work out. The testing went well and right before her final test, Lori told Dad and Mom what she was doing. Dad and Mom were overwhelmed with excitement and gratitude with what they heard.

It was thrilling to think that the end of Dad's struggle was potentially within reach. Thankfully, in June 2005, Lori passed her final test, and the doctors gave the okay to schedule the kidney transplant. The transplant surgery was scheduled for August 19, 2005. We all waited with great anticipation for that day to arrive. With such good news, it made being voted into the All-Star Game that much better.

Just when it looked like everything was going smoothly, my dad had a terrible health scare the Sunday before the All-Star Game. It was planned that most of my family would attend the All-Star Game. However, Dad had to remain at home because of his dialysis. It was around midnight and I was driving to the airport to fly to Detroit. As usual, I called home to check-in with my parents. Little did I know that this call would save my dad's life.

My brother Ken Eckstein with his law school friends Lori Vaughan (right) and Tracy Dreispul (left)

Mom had fallen asleep because she had an early morning flight. Dad picked up the phone and said, "David, I can't breathe! Here's your mother." With that Dad tossed the phone onto the bed. Mom woke up and picked up the phone. "What's going on?" I asked her. "Dad says he can't breathe." My mom replied, "I don't know!" So, I told her to call 911. Mom promptly hung up and called 911. Then I called my sister Christine who lives across the street from my parents, and told her, "Mom just called 911 on Dad. You better get over there."

Christine went straight over to my parents' house and began talking to my dad telling him "to be strong." A few minutes later my father went unconscious. By the time I was able to reach Christine on the phone, the last thing I heard was, "He's unconscious! Pray!" Dad was experiencing congestive heart failure because his lungs were full of fluid.

Thankfully, the paramedics arrived quickly, revived Dad, and transported him straight to the hospital. I got the news that

Dad was stable and breathing just before my plane for Detroit took off. My father remained in the hospital for the next six days with my mom by his side. We were told that had another 10 minutes elapsed, Dad would have died. Dad made a full recovery and, remarkably, this episode did not postpone the transplant scheduled in August.

Photo courtesy of Amy Mikler

Seeing his grandchilden grow up gave Whitey the heart to survive.

44

Jamie Squire/Getty Images

With my father's condition under control, I was able to turn my focus back to the All-Star Game. I was especially pleased that my brother Rick was able to join me at the game as a bullpen catcher. It was a special night.

On August 19, 2005, my father's fight with kidney failure ended with a successful transplant operation. Lori's kidney began working immediately. What a miracle of life! Dad continues to get stronger and healthier every day. We are all grateful to Lori for her selfless gift.

There were several newspaper and television reports about Dad's transplant, and the fans of St. Louis took my parents to heart. This was evident when my parents landed in St. Louis to watch me play live for the first time as a Cardinal. They came to watch the final regular season series of 2005 and the closing ceremony of Busch Stadium. As soon as they stepped off the plane, people began approaching them with words of endearment. People recognized them from the news reports, and my parents were overwhelmed with the outpouring of warmth showed toward them. Even at the games, people came up to my parents with well wishes. My parents and I will never forget the kindness and support they received from the Cardinal fans.

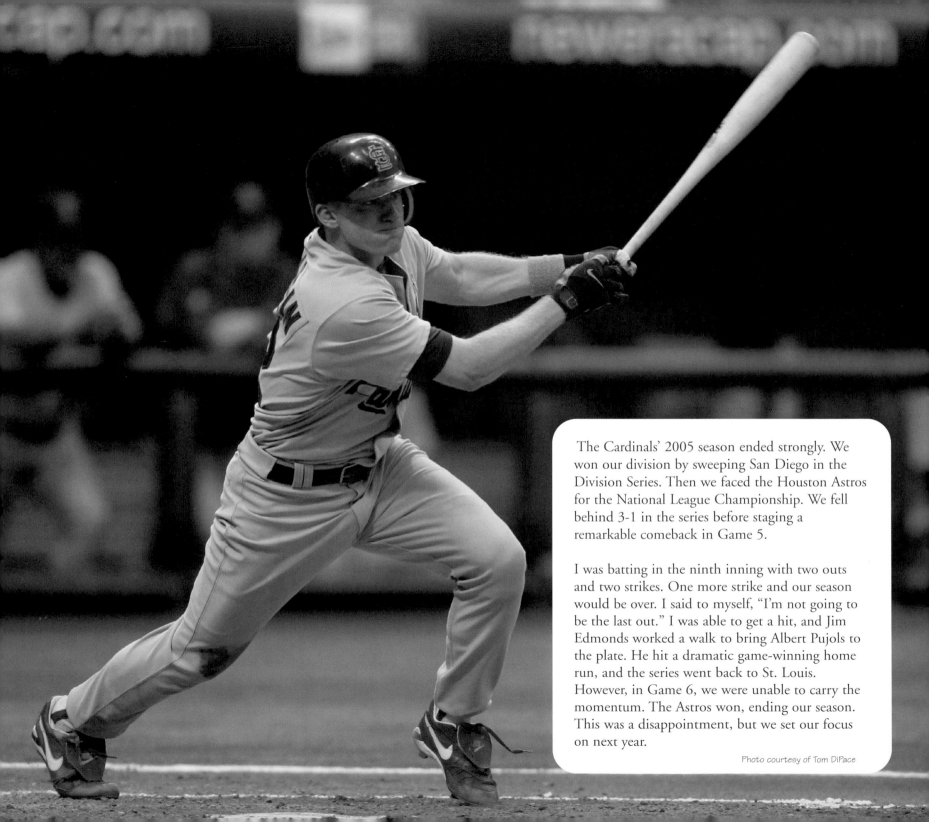

The Cardinals' 2005 season ended strongly. We won our division by sweeping San Diego in the Division Series. Then we faced the Houston Astros for the National League Championship. We fell behind 3-1 in the series before staging a remarkable comeback in Game 5.

I was batting in the ninth inning with two outs and two strikes. One more strike and our season would be over. I said to myself, "I'm not going to be the last out." I was able to get a hit, and Jim Edmonds worked a walk to bring Albert Pujols to the plate. He hit a dramatic game-winning home run, and the series went back to St. Louis. However, in Game 6, we were unable to carry the momentum. The Astros won, ending our season. This was a disappointment, but we set our focus on next year.

The 2005 offseason was monumental for me. On November 26, 2005, I married Ashley Drane in All Souls Catholic Church. All Souls is very special to me because it is my hometown church where I had received the sacraments of baptism, penance, communion and confirmation. The wedding was beautiful, and the celebration continued at our reception held in the Yacht and Beach Club Resort at Walt Disney World. We enjoyed a wonderful honeymoon in Hawaii.

After the honeymoon, we went to Memphis, Tennessee, to enjoy time with my in-laws, Tony and Sharon Drane, and my brother and sisters in-law, Michael, Tara and Taylor. I am blessed that my family has grown.

Photo courtesy of Tom DiPace

Going into the 2006 season, the Cardinals had high expectations as a club. We started strong in April and May and established ourselves as the frontrunner for the Central Division. However, each season poses different challenges, and this season's challenge was overcoming injuries suffered by the starting lineup.

My first injury was dealing with a concussion. I took a knee to the head while sliding into second base. My next injury occurred in a collision at home plate that tore my oblique muscle from the bone. I was placed on the disabled list (DL) where only time could help heal my injury. I had to stop hitting, stop throwing, and reduce my workouts. There was nothing I could do to get better faster.

Elsa/Getty Images

Time was the only cure, and there was no timetable set for when I would be able to return. I was fearful that I wouldn't have the opportunity to get back on the field before the end of the season. I was especially frustrated that I couldn't help my team during the critical month of September. Thanks to the expertise of the Cardinals' trainers, I was able to get over the final hump with 10 games left to play. On the third day back, once again I injured myself. I hit a ball thinking it was a double. As I rounded first base, I felt a pull in my left hamstring. Fortunately it was only a strain that allowed me to play the final weekend of the season.

Many people discounted the Cardinals and did not factor in the size of our hearts coming into the playoffs. We knew we were at our strongest. The team was finally healthy, and we had something to prove.

49

Our first test was against the San Diego Padres. An important moment happened in the bottom of the sixth inning of Game 1 with San Diego at bat. The Padres had the bases loaded and there were two outs. The batter hit a sure base hit, but out of nowhere in short right field, Ronnie Belliard, our second baseman, made a spectacular diving play throwing the runner out at first base. It was one of the best plays I have ever seen by a second baseman. I believe this play was the turning point that created the momentum for us to defeat the Padres and become the Division Series Champions.

Our next test was the New York Mets. We knew this was going to be a tough challenge. The Mets had one of the most feared offenses in the game of baseball. However, our pitchers rose to the challenge, creating a back-and-forth series. Game 5 was especially tough for me. I sprained my left shoulder in the first inning. Then in the eighth, I bruised my throwing fingers as I tried to lay down a suicide squeeze. This is something I was definitely going to have to deal with because I was not going to let it stop me from playing the rest of the series.

Game 7 was a classic with great pitching, unbelievable defense and timely hitting. Yadier Molina's two-run homer to break a 1-1 tie in the top of the ninth inning and Adam Wainwright striking out the final Met hitter with the bases loaded finalized our trip to the World Series.

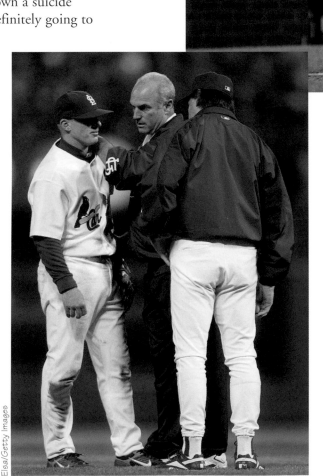

Trainer Barry Weinberg and Manager Tony LaRussa check me out after injuring my shoulder in Game 5 against the Mets.

The World Series began in Detroit because the American League won the All-Star Game. So, our team began the series on the road. Many considered us the underdogs, and some sarcastically said the Tigers would take us in three games. Once again they discounted our heart and this proved only to motivate us more bringing the club closer together. Our focus was on one thing: becoming the World Series Champions.

The series got off to a good start by us winning Game 1. But we knew we had a hard series ahead of us. Detroit proved this by defeating us in Game 2. As we headed back to St. Louis tied one game each, we looked forward to playing the next three games in front of our home fans.

Game 3 was dominated by Chris Carpenter. He pitched eight scoreless innings and led us to an important victory. We were down in Game 4, but we didn't give up. We fell behind 3-0 early on, but we found a way to battle back. This game will go on to be one of the most memorable for me. I was 4 for 5, had three doubles, and two RBI's — one of which was the game winner.

As we entered Game 5, we knew we had an opportunity to become World Series Champions in front of our loyal fans in our new stadium. We wanted to take full advantage of this opportunity. The offense was able to do just enough, but the real story was our pitching. Jeff Weaver set the tone of the game by pitching eight masterful innings. Then Adam Wainwright secured our World Series championship by pitching a scoreless ninth.

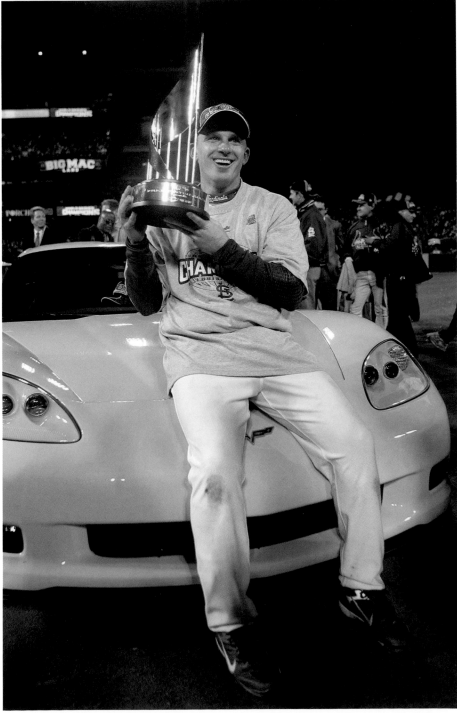

As soon as the final out was made, I screamed, threw my hands in the air, and ran over to Belliard. Then, Belliard and I ran to jump into the player pile. It was an incredible moment. During the celebration, someone from Major League Baseball told me that I had been selected MVP but not to say anything until it was announced. I was stunned. I had dreamed all of my life of winning a World Series championship, but I never dreamed of becoming a World Series MVP. During the ceremony, I stood awestruck as Commissioner Bud Selig awarded me the MVP trophy and then I was handed the keys to a brand new Chevrolet Corvette. This was my first new car ever. As I think back on the series and of all the players who rose to the occasion, I am humbled to have this honor bestowed on me and am proud to be on this team that has heart.

MVP Stats

.364 batting average (8 for 22)
4 RBIs
3 doubles
3 runs scored

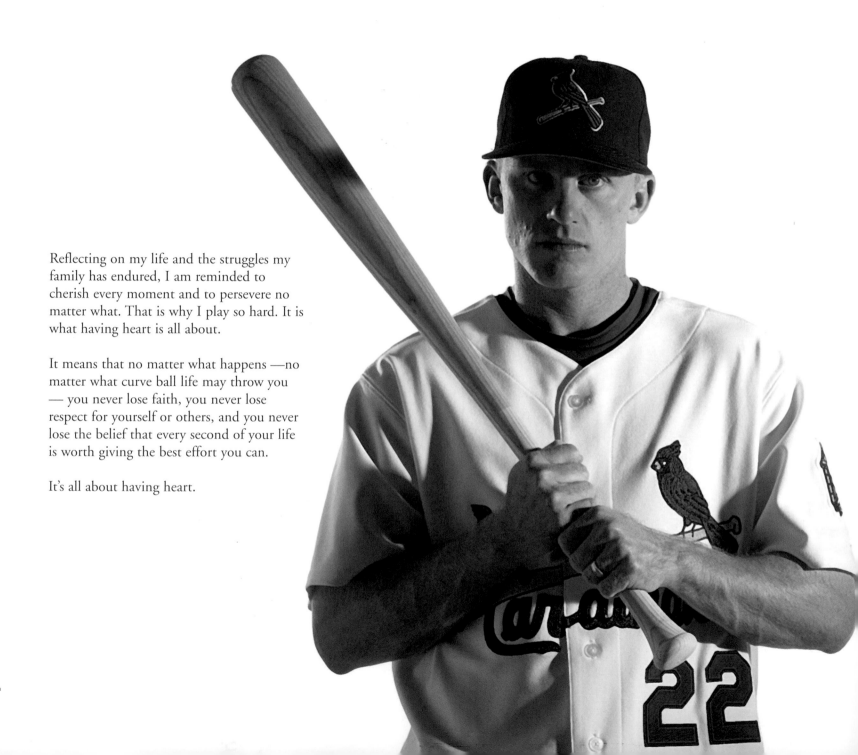

Reflecting on my life and the struggles my family has endured, I am reminded to cherish every moment and to persevere no matter what. That is why I play so hard. It is what having heart is all about.

It means that no matter what happens —no matter what curve ball life may throw you — you never lose faith, you never lose respect for yourself or others, and you never lose the belief that every second of your life is worth giving the best effort you can.

It's all about having heart.

Transplant Updates

Susan Eckstein Gaines received a living donor kidney from her mother, Pat, on November 29, 1988, at Shands Hospital in Gainesville, Florida. She graduated from the University of Florida with a B.H.S. in Rehabilitative Counseling (1994) and a M.A. in Counselor Education (1997). She married Frederic Gaines in 1999 and has two children, Elise and Ricky. Susan has worked as an academic advisor for both the University of Central Florida and University of South Florida. Currently, she is pursuing her elementary education teaching certification.

Pat Eckstein donated her kidney to her daughter, Susan, on November 29, 1988. She taught elementary school for 32 years and is currently serving as the Reading Coach for Bentley Elementary in Sanford, Florida. In addition to her husband and children, Pat enjoys the support from her mother, Jo Biondi, and her uncle, Pat Biondi, of New York City.

Ken Eckstein received a cadaveric donor kidney on July 26, 1991, at Shands Hospital in Gainesville, Florida. He graduated from the University of Florida with a B.A. in English (1992) and a Juris Doctorate with honors (1998) from the University of Florida College of Law. He worked as a Staff Attorney for both the State Circuit Court and the Florida Supreme Court. Ken is currently pursuing a career as a writer and painter.

Christine Eckstein received a cadaveric donor kidney on July 30, 1991 at Shands Hospital in Gainesville, Florida. She graduated from the University of Florida with her B.A. in Political Science (1993) and a Juris Doctorate with honors (1996) from the University of Florida College of Law. Christine married Peter Schoemann in 1996 and has four children, Kate', David, Kenny, and Ava. She has worked for Gulf Coast Legal Services, and currently is an active stay-at-home mom nurturing her children especially her two autistic sons.

Whitey Eckstein received a living donor kidney from family friend, Lori Vaughan, on August 19, 2005, at Florida Hospital in Orlando, Florida. Whitey is recently retired after 35 years of teaching and serving 16 years as a Sanford City Commissioner. He is healthy and enjoying retirement with his six grandchildren and three English Springer Spaniels, Gaby, Rudy and Charlie.

Lori Vaughan donated her kidney to Whitey Eckstein on August 19, 2005, at Florida Hospital in Orlando, Florida. She is corporate bankruptcy attorney for Foley & Lardner and returned to work only two weeks after the surgery. Lori currently lives in New York City.

DONATION STATISTICS

More than 91,000 men, women and children currently await life-saving transplants.

Every 12 minutes another name is added to the national transplant waiting list.

An average of 18 people die each day from the lack of available organs for transplant.

In 2005, there were 7,593 deceased organ donors and 6,895 living organ donors resulting in 28,108 organ transplants.

In 2005, U.S. transplant banks made available 44,000 human organs/tissue for transplantation.

Approximately 1,000,000 tissue transplants are performed annually.

For the latest donation and transplantation data, information and statistics visit the UNOS Website WWW.UNOS.ORG.

FOR MORE INFORMATION ON BECOMING AN ORGAN DONOR, PLEASE VISIT WWW.DONATELIFE.NET